Honey and Lime

"Honey and Lime," by Peggy Carr. ISBN 1-58939-893-9.

Library of Congress Control Number: 2006928554

Manufactured in the United States of America.

Honey and Lime

Peggy Carr

To Irwin, in celebration of almost
forty years of friendship

Acknowledgements

I wish to thank the many people who have supported my efforts at writing over the years, including my friends and relatives at home and abroad whose love and confidence continue to inspire me.

Thanks to Aloma Williams, Jeana Noel and Kathy Sloane for responding so readily when I called for help.

My deep appreciation to Opal Palmer Adisa for taking the time to read the manuscript and for her insights and encouragement.

I owe much to Dr. Cecil Cyrus and his wife Kathryn who were courageous enough to take a chance many years ago on an impetuous teenager from a remote rural village.

To my friends John Horne and Irwin Martin, thank you for giving credence to my dreams.

Thanks to my daughter Vashti for her patience in helping to prepare the manuscript and for understanding my many moods when I'm absorbed in my writing. A special thank you to my son Nicky, who helps to maintain my faith in the men of his generation. I wish also to thank my foster daughter Nichole Bennett and my niece Dahlia Deane, who both enabled me to expand my concept of motherhood.

There are no words to adequately convey my pure gratitude to my mother, Leila Deane, who has always known and has shown me what matters most.

Table of Contents

Today

Today I woke up
and said
YES
to the morning
today
breakfast was a breeze
and my clothes
dressed me
today
I smiled in traffic
and waved
at crazy drivers
today
cameras and tripods
waltzed to my touch
today
I told history
to the children
and laughed
today
music dripped
from my wrists
today
a poem was born
in joy
today
I knew I was loved

Moving

Once again I tear pieces
off my self
trying to unglue from
one more place
gather souvenir bits of
shrapnel from another spent cycle
mix a fresh palette of
aspirations
and head for
the monochrome horizon

Journey

Journey broken
but no fountain
for my thirst

strangers
crowd my shoulders

dust only
in the distance

no destination

yet
I must take me to
completion
to transition
whole
undefiled

I too passed this way

or is it...

I passed this way too

New Life

Wide as the oceans of my birth
and innocent
I embrace the tide that races
to my unexplored recesses
and swirls there
endlessly

Astonishment alights each morning
as I harvest new strength from
the depths of each night

Half-heartedly I scan the signposts of
my past
but like ancient fallen tombstones
they have no bearing on
my expanse of joy

Alone and pure
a new love recreates me

Flight of the Firstborn

He streaks past his sixteenth year
small island life stretched tight
across his shoulders
his strides rehearsing city blocks
college brochures
airline schedules
stream excitedly through his
newly competent hands
his goodbyes like blurred neon
on a morning suddenly gone wet

I'm left stranded
on a tiny patch of time
still reaching
to wipe the cereal from his smile

Letting Go

The birthing is never over
Our wombs still heave and
scream
as we deliver them
repeatedly
into the hand of strangers
anxiety a blood rush through
the swiftly unravelling cord of
their dependence
pride a pulse spiking at
their innocent freedom cry

The sterile snip of closing doors
belies the anguish
of composure stitched tight by
clichéd assurances
A mass of nurturing routines
flops discarded on
the cold steel of
inevitability
Our weeping breasts
stain swathes of pristine hours

To My Mother

Isn't it strange how
I no longer fit
on your lap
my head's too tall
for your bosom
and a whole lot of
physics
deny my swinging
from your waist

yet
now like never before
I'm clasped to your
dreams
the relentless love rhythms
of your heartbeat
fill my ear
and some days
I slide sickeningly
again and again
down your old
disappointments

It's watching my daughter
grow up
that does it

Foreign Find

Slender stream of
honeyed light
stretching rainbows through
mists of strange sounds
dances lithely with
my own flame
subtle strength
bending my smile
again
and again

Church 1

A sturdy ageless little hill
her threadbare skirt of
trees
spread wide in constant curtsey
to the spray-soaked wind
the thin path slipping
carelessly off her shoulder a
coy reminder of
her old affair
with the sea

She had lured his hues
the rough strength of
his dark rocks to
her green expanses
nourished them on solitude and
the myriad flavours of
light and shade poured
daily by the sun
until the church rose
reaching for the nurturing sky
a sanctuary sublime
austere
serene
despite the sea
reminding her...
reminding her...

Retro Night

Our night wore mostly black

velvet gowns sequined with
fireflies
or swirling skirts of sable rain
Sometimes sultry in charcoal gray with
pearls
she'd cling coquettishly to
shirttails of a tired day
and entice the lemon fragrance from
the sacks of grass we snuggled

But she looked her best in silver with
magenta
and moved like she knew it
ignoring the insolence of
kerosene lamps that dared to
wink at her
from beneath the thatch

That's when we'd try to steal
her wild perfumes
and douse her with the hale aroma of
roasting corns

when we'd toss her armfuls of
homegrown songs
and dance ecstatic
as she tossed them back
when grandma's stories would feather
our skins

their rhythm and cadence
weighting our heads
so we'd never hear our night
whisper her surrender to the dawn

Note To The Unseen

Tear me a piece of morning
pristine
crisp
unwrapped from a silver sunrise
mix me a few pastel notes of
birdsong
toss me a fine brush of
ocean spray
and I'll paint you a wet poem
and lean it against
a new Caribbean sky
to dry

Moods Of Destiny

She
> languid
> wide
> offering exotic gifts
> and scents
> from her far mountain home

He
> quick
> restless
> lover of shores
> now runs abandoned
> into her endless fluidity
> whispering secrets he has carried
> patiently from other worlds

She
> escapes to his infinity
> rests on his wide horizons

He
> slowly unravels his foam-crusted
> tension
> surrenders his saline strength

And sometimes

She
       rushes crazed
       to his massive heaving
       her passion staining his mood
       to dark turmoil

He
       arches mightily
       straddling her boundaries
       curving their mingled delirium to
       a towering primal protest of
       unlikely love

Yet
       always
       eventually
       the river meets the sea

Wino

I wonder
if he
knows
that
champagne
flows
from his
fingertips
and lips

He must
know
though
or why
would he
pour so
sparingly
to me

Affair

Shadows
on a magic moonscape
shifting
at his breath
converge
and melt
into each other's
darkness
without a whisper

Wisps
of days
all tangled up
in aching dreams
and
shards of night
piled high
waiting
to ignite
against his eyes'
hot touch

Somewhere
in the spirals
of a phone
my silent scream
condenses
in
the deep warm
colours
of his voice

When He Went Away

I packed his cases full of
cotton shirts
and thick warm nights
while he carefully
arranged his promises
in the windows of our future

Reverently I touched that morning
when he left
his farewell trailing
from a plane
and blending with
the chaste white fingers of
cooksmoke
which stole upward
through the dew to
wipe the smudges from the sky

How cheerfully our love moved out
to live inside
a cold blue envelope
and like an orphaned street-wise
child
slept easily
between two thin indifferent
lines

Like sheathed claws
atop a taut silk sheet
his first lies probed

the boundaries
of my innocence
then
artfully his words
rehearsed to
a finer edge
until
winter
riots
strikes
and
government
flicked smoothly from his pen
to quiver
in my hopes

Carelessly he tried to patch
my still-hot pain
with random ten pound notes
and pictures
of some grey defiant
stranger

My letters drifted into
slow soliloquy
and reassured themselves
like Job

A velvet tongue of
tired midnight breeze
licked the moisture from
my cheeks
then shook an old newssheet

awake
snuggled underneath
and belched the flavour of
too many lonely women
on its breath

Today I forgot to
tremble
to the rhythm
of the postman's
bell

Dream

He rode in on my tiredness
wrapped in cool grey
mist
but donned his colours
smoothly
once safely past
the first minute

My secrets welcomed him
with showers
of amorphous thoughts
and bits of bright
reality

He fused them all
and molded them
exquisitely
to build one simple
graphic want

Then morning struck
and cruelly
despoiled his art

Song Of A Weary Wanderer

If I could only rest
for one night

if I could anchor
my anger
and rest
for one night
hushed
in the calm of someone's eyes

if I could unbuckle
my doubts
and rest
for one night
fed
on the homegrown truth
of someone's song

if I could unzip
my suspicions
and rest
for one night
clean
under the sincere passion
of someone's hands

if I could untie
my past
and rest
for one night

scented
in the delicate wisdom
of someone's mind

if I could switch off
my arguments
and rest
for one night
warm
in the soft glow
of someone's understanding

if I could only rest
for one night
safe
in the shelter
of someone's love
I know I'll be strong enough
to walk
naked
into tomorrow

Liar

I wish you
wouldn't
wear
the same
lie
every evening
Can't you see
it's tearing
just
where
the boys
keep holding
you back
with *a drop*
and *a game of*
dominoes

I Miss You

I miss you
when....
the first grey light
of dawn
slips into your side
of bed
and reminds me that
I'm cold

I miss you
when.....
my silly jokes
slide back into hiding
and my laughter
bounces off
the startled silence

I miss you
when.....
my tears go chasing
after some elusive song
that seems to hold
your voice.....

....and my arms
can't understand
the empty space between them

I miss you
when.....
a cardboard copy
of your eyes
soaks up my smile.....

....and you can't hear
me breathe the moonlight

I miss you
when.....
my thoughts refuse
to climb aboard
my spoken words
insisting
that they'd only crash
among the aliens.....

.....and no one knows
that I am silent

I miss you
when.....
I shuffle home
chained
to a massive day
and I can't reach
the lips
that would unshackle me

I miss you
when.....
all of you
comes pouring through
my ear
and all of me
is answering....

....and I can't make you
climb out of the phone

I miss you
when.....
your chest beneath my
cheek
dissolves
into a pillow
and sleep ignores my
ardent plea
to reverse that
cruel trick.....

....and my hands forget
that now
the night brings only
shadows

I miss you....

....always

Thoughts

Thoughts
that never quite slip past
the stern guard of
reality
sometimes
steal a rest
upon the contours of
my face
and
leak their secret
to his nonchalant
eyes

Thoughts
gleaming proud with
decorations
for valor against fate
now
scatter helplessly
before the white slash
of his smile

Thoughts
hold to the dream
that waits
crouched
between our conversations
knowing it will die
starved thin
across the bare

and arid
nights

Final Chores

If the sum of
all our years
should come to this
one kiss
mustn't I gather
every bereft minute of
the approaching days
to the furnace of
your lips
mustn't I inscribe the volume
of my surplus passion on
your shoulders
and heap the recalcitrant
memories
high against your chest
as we smelt
us
down to one last goodbye

Call Me Thus...

Come...
    and I'll be gentle
    when I peel your lips apart
    until I hear your need

Come...
    and I'll be gentle
    when I sink my love
    into your soul and
    drain its lonely tears

Come...
    and I'll be gentle
    when I smash the boundaries
    of your vision
    and flood your world with dreams

Come...
    and I'll be gentle
    when I thread my gaze
    on yours and pull
    the joy into your eyes

Come...
    and I'll be gentle
    with my fingers
    in your hair
    and my footsteps
    on your life

Reflection

Yes
it was that day
that I found
glinting
among our sharp grey
quarrels
and wished that
I could keep

that day when
I wore only
the single strand
of promise that
shimmered
in your sleep-encrusted
voice
and our ardour
leapt
into the morning
splashing new colours
on the sun

and we unwrapped
my fears
decided they were
worthless
and sunk them
in our brand new
confidence
and leisurely

we explored
the corners of your
silence
and you let me hold
your visions
gently
for a while

and laughter danced between us

It was that day
that made me say
I'd stay

Nightwatch

Sleep
like a frightened child
cowers
far from the images that
frolic
in an ever-swelling dam of
tears
pain
implacable
in evening wear
persuades
the night to linger
while
she dances
wantonly
with my frail
young
courage

A new star
panics
as my prayers
sneak
past it
a few eccentric
raindrops
stammer some excuse
for
not bringing
any

answers

Slowly
laboriously
I crumple my anguish
and
toss it into the
encroaching
dawn

Once Only

Her young face
knelt
her eyes unfurled and
waiting
like new lilies
on a rain-promised morning
to cup the first warm
sprinkle
of his desire

but he tossed instead
his scorn
at her shy unclothed
anthem
then cringed
trapped inside his own
astonishment
as her life broke
into a million ripples
and never yet again stood still
long enough for
his image to
alight

Duel By Night

Her chest was frail
beneath his foot
but her grit
climbed easily
up the cold spike of
his stare

She sneaked a draught
of air
from a rancid place
between his toes
and tried to hook
her pity
on his soul

His fear hurried
through his leg
ricocheted
against her mouth
and escaped
in a hot red spurt

The night lay flat
against her eyes
and trembled

Feebly now
she groped again
to find
to touch
the wound in him
for which he sought

to steal her breath
as balm

Like a crazed outrider
his laughter hurtled
past her ear

the blade
composed and silent
rode imperiously
behind

The rocks beneath her back
grew friendly

She poured her only smile
into his flaming
eyes
as her patient right hand
bared its secret
and her questions
hitchhiked
to the ether
on slivers
of sudden thunder

Like an exiled conductor
she implores his empty eyes
the empty sky
as the enigma's motif
plays eerily
why
why

Over The Edge

The pain hacks at
the anchors on her brain
anger
darts through her senses
exploding every quiet space
splattering
fragments of her mind
against an unyielding
fear

In helpless frenzy
she clutches
at wildly flying relics
of herself
stumbles
on a broken laugh
that fell from the pages
of some ancient comic book

Her voice creaks to
a half-remembered stance
and tries to lift
the laughter gently
but that too explodes
and rips the silence
from the night

Her eyes fumble
with odd pieces of
a charred

inverted
world
as the darkness grows bold
and struts around
inside her head

Genesis Of A Warrior

She fluttered to the edge of
womanhood
and poised there
waiting
for that first touch
of life
to dry her moist new
eyes

He too was poised

and waiting

With practised ease
his smile closed over her
and his bored promises
held her still
while the strangely empty
days
tore her wings off

Slowly he impaled her
on his ego
mopping her thin protests
with thick wads of
reassurances

His amusement soared
at her brief pathetic struggle
to assert herself
but his interest quickly
collapsed

inside her bruised silence

He left her for dead
in a congealing pool of
her own disgust
and his indifference
hitched his smile in place
and moved on

Gingerly at first
and then in bold blue-black
swarms
the anger settled
in her eyes

and the steel grew
in huge scabs on her heart

The years covered her in silence

Now
down the centre lane of
life
astride a tall resolve
rides a warrior

on her patrol
the unfledged thrive
while their would-be spoilers
surrender
sharp practised smiles
under the steady double-barreled
knowledge in her eyes

Womanland

Woman
I know the colour of
of your laughter....
was it not painted
by the light
in the eyes of your child
as he hugged your knees

and those tears.....
didn't they leak through
the sometimes tremulous dam
of your courage
when his father's love
died on you

And that hunger
for someone
anyone
to understand
and care.....
I know it roams
the desert of your silence
by day
and claws its cage
inside your chest
at night

Did I touch your hands.....
maybe not

but I know their trembling
magic
of coaxing
sparse ephemeral dollars
to cover
the ever-bulging needs of
loved ones
I know those unique badges
won in countless battles
with troops of laundry
and armed only
with brown soap
and cold water

and how often those same hands
like robust yang-yang trees
have soaked the night in
sweetness
and fitted it snugly
inch by inch
upon a lovers frame

And haven't you shyly turned
the pages of your inner soul
for a bright-eyed man
who looked
and laughed excitedly
because he thought
they'd make good paper planes....
yet you'll turn those pages
again
one day
and hope that this time

this one
is literate

And sometimes sick and worn
you've been tended
by the anxious amateur eyes of
your toddlers
and some venerable home-remedy
that rally behind your
will
to fight the spectre of
your empty purse

But when you explore....
your feet curled
above the solid ground
your heart made benevolent
by the life
spawned in its shade
a smile weaving softly
through the tapestry of
aspirations in your eyes
do you know that
you're a creator
of worlds
of dreams
of children to fill them

You see
I know you think
you're in a strange harsh land
but

THIS
is Womanland

here....
take my hand....

Fickle River

Her vast indifferent face
swallows my frantic eyes
reaches for my screams
my incoherent questions
sliding
down a shrug of
her sluggish shoulders

She shivers in distaste
at the disturbed air
around my protesting limbs
nonchalantly catches the
early light
contorting past my
shoulders
throws it downstream
and slaps a casual
invitation
at my feet

From the glut of
colourful gossip
she snatches bits like
crazy
pressure
jilted
lonely
floats them past
my ear
sneers wetly

at my confusion

Yesterday I loved her

I loved her dark profundity
her playful skittering
when threatened
by the wind
her artist's impression
of my morning face
her serene soul
that patiently
unlocked my head
each day
and emptied all its tensions

Yesterday I loved her

Today she took my sister

She Lives

More than most women
she is
wonderful and wise
and has courage
more than most women
she is
free of men's passions
and strong
more than most women
she is
generous and warm
and laughs
more than most women
she is gentle and profound
and forgives
more than most women
she is
intuitive and calm
and sings
more than most women
she is
the occasional dream of
all our wistful selves

One-Legged Man

A thousand journeys trek across
his face
over ridges of crystallized
courage
down dry tear-beds
now lined with dust from
young graves
His mouth trembles to
hold shut on
four hundred years of
force-fed shame

A thousand journeys crisscross
his dreams
immigrations and deportations
to and from someone clse's
agenda
Hands balled into play-rewind
he battles an ancient monster
cloned down the centuries
to warp his destiny
on shore after shore

A thousand journeys crunch
under his stick
his offbeat progress
in perfect counterpoint to
the smooth roll of his future
repeating itself each day
from his front door
to the corner shop

49

Shake

Roots man from the start
he wrapped his country in
his head
tied his culture
in his blood
and roamed the mountains of
his music

Artist to the bone
he crafted words from
broken mirrors and belly pain
to build mosaic homelandscapes
and sentient
unerring portraits

Surgeon with a pen
he excised scars from
old colonial wounds
infused lines with
core Vincentian colour
transplanting his
heart rhythms to
the page

Voyager to the end
I write love poems now
he said

*(Dedicated to the memory of Ellsworth
Shake Keane, 1927 to 1997)*

Tragedy

The rain leaned back
against the thick cushion of
the night
and waited until
history was scrawled
in long uncertain loops
across its slick black
face
then it hastened to
the ever-distance
and hid the legend
there

We had tears for breakfast

The sea ignored the
angry stutter of some strange
impotent gull
the soft pleas of
many patient boats
and ancient mother
that she is
tucked her thirteen children in
to eternity
and closed the blinds

Our sorrow stood
on tiptoe
to touch even those
we never knew

and each day wore
the same limp
unwashed light

Someone painted eight new
stars
on our Vincentian sky

*(Dedicated to the memory of the
thirteen people, including eight
Vincentians, who were aboard LIAT
Flight 319 when it disappeared on
August 4, 1986.)*

On Higher Ground

Where shall I walk
now
I've outgrown the hills
I once carved

What shall I plant
now
I've broken the fences of
seasons and time

What shall I sing
now
my voice has surpassed the
range of chants it once raised

For whom shall I care
now
my heart has unfurled
to boundless capacity

Perhaps I'll find me a mountain
tall enough for giants
where planting season rests
and the harvesting songs of
triumphant women soar
amidst the rustling of busy hearts
dispensing love to all the children of
the universe

*(Dedicated to the memory of Earlene
Horne, 1949 to 1998)*

Carribean-ites

Some god-ling must have smiled
and others wept
as the sun spewed us
from her eventful womb
then abandoned us

laughing

as we drowned
in the sweat of shackled
arms
and plump white smiles

sleeping

while we crawled
like wingless moths
from fear to fear

But the good earth listened
as we ploughed our blood
into her dark bosom
and she hid our heroes
in graves piled high
with old convictions
made new
in the mill of years
and need

Slowly Damballah perished
across the steep slopes of
new minds
strewn with tall black
pride
and words

Are we not strong enough
now
to step out of our own footprints
on our many shores
and reach to draw
a single new horizon

My Castle

Inside the castle of
my dream
there are no hollow
words
no worn-out promises
feasting
at long tables of
forgiveness

There are no egos
armed with
infidelity
and thick shields of
tradition
standing guard on
precocious rulers

No working shifts of
trained lies
hover attentively
to skim the
meaning
from each alliance
There are no thrones
of pride
to which love
must pay court

No hordes of
bland excuses

muster daily
to defend the creed
of incompetence

No flags of sexual
conquest
fly
from tall boastings
no crest of
ownership
adorns the doors

Inside the castle of
my dream
the naked self
knows freedom
in its exile

Bullfighter

Swollen voices
chains of faces
enclose your life
shut sweetness from the air

half a ton of
malevolent problems
breathes your space
the chant goes up
for you to twirl
to fly
to make the moves
streak the colours
shape the light
spin the world
while the side-liners
scream
more
encore

But the thunder
in your chest
is your solitary heart
the sweat in your eyes
is not for sale
and the blood knows only
the desolate tracks
down the contours
of your frame

Yes
you were born
clutching a cape
but you also carry a dream
of someone
who will clear the ring
change the music
take your hand
and ask you to dance
instead

Woman To Woman

Silence waits like a polite beggar
outside your door
for scraps of your sometimes mundane
days
then as if guilty at your charity
he unobtrusively
patches the odd quarrel
swabs the constantly spilling voices
of the children
neatly folds your spontaneous songs
and tucks them out of sight

How smoothly he insinuates
to become a favourite guest
mocking gently
at your furtive pen
then a bold lover
who snuffs out your flickering
lines
spreads a thick bed of excuses
smothers your whispered prayers
and once more commits incest
on our generation

for didn't he grow from
those interminable rows
where our grandmothers planted
their words daily

with the yams
and didn't our mothers learn
to nurture him
like a prodigy
amidst a profusion of
male opinions and demands

Outraged
I now stalk to your door
revile your beggar
insult your guest
depose your lover
invade your silence

My sanction is his presence

On The Outside

When they drew the line
did they have me in mind
Did they think that
I
would try to climb
their thick cold
skin
or long to be inside

Did they think that
I
would hold my need
outstretched
before me
and rattle discordant
smiles
as they toss me
cold leftovers of
their murderous past

If they should ever find
a crack in their fear
through which they
could peer
they would see
that my bare feet
fit snugly in the earth
that the sun
runs
happily through my pores

frolics in my eyes
and sleeps in my heart

They would see
my hands
giving life to this land
and every tree
under which I stand
bowing low
to shelter me

They would see me
rise
from the mist of my
indulgent seas
and curve eagerly
into the familiar arms
of the wind
which slips the ocean from
my shoulders
and unashamedly
worships
this naked skin

When they built
their walls
and wired them
with lies
did they think
that *my* children
would inherit
their jails

No Quarter

I will not apologise
for knowing who I am
for being born woman
will not abandon my vision
or cage my ambition
I do not vacillate
or accommodate
cannot barter my integrity
or femininity
in exchange for comfort
or trust

I know
friendships may not survive
and love might vapourize
under the fire of my credo
but in *my* life
I forge the principles

Normal

Don't try to
sell me normal
cause that's
all twisted up
hanging
upside down
puking
its insides
onto itself

The Box

Do you think that your tags
identify me
affixing a label
makes you know me

Categorizing only gives you safety
from ever having to see me

Tagged
numbered
measured
coloured
gendered
the me of me
is still a mystery

And what if I do my
cross-gender
cosmo
act

What does that do
to your neatly pigeon-holed
response box

Church 2

Walls stuffed
hot with hallelujahs
bleached with self-righteousness
shut out the stink of
poverty
pressed up against the
window panes

Consciences plunge headlong
into rivers of Jesus-blood
Amens roll mercilessly over
prostrate wills

Volume is imbued with virtue
Sins consigned to the faceless
unsaved
Heaven dangles
like a lottery prize
Hell cracks over the backs of
stragglers

God is offered
withheld
maligned
infused with every whim
in every shade of
opinion
and psychosis

Charity sits smugly
for a day
on collection plates

Coward

I'm told …

… how provincial of me to shiver
and cringe in horror from
coils of hate rearing to
strike
at every decent soul

… what a wimp I am to cry
as I watch remnants of
a country's young
scraped
contemptuously
from marauding boots

… only a weakling vomits
at the stench of
disemboweled consciences
at the rot of
villainy
like putrid entrails
twined about a nation's throat
in daily murder-suicide ritual

I say …

… I must flee this underworld of
sophistry

I Find Them

I find them everywhere

orphaned by indifference
clinging to the rocky crevices
of adolescence

floating like jetsam
in polluted streams of
politics

bound on alters of
greed
sacrificed to
obscene gods

trapped in the lairs of
predators wearing the skins of
fathers

We slither in futility
as they reach with
stubs of amputated trust
trying to clutch my vision of
their efficacy

Still I find them

Like vacant strip dancers

pinned in the gaudy lights
of adult lust
peeling dignity
stripping ambition
snapping the girdle of
self-worth
seeking some crumb of
acclaim

Like a frantic weaver
in lost Eden
I juggle strands of
music
art
love
to cover them
but often
I'm too late
too slow
too alone

I bleed again
into the ever-thirsty gutters
of my land

We Talk

(Dedicated to the youth of my country)

Country Talk

We box up like banana in
cardboard values still
stamp England pon de side
trying fuh mek root pon ah
scraps ah land wedge in
between deep deep
South America water
ah we door mouth
and stinging nettle Bush
like fire
in we back yard
too much mouth fuh feed
too little voice fuh
anybody hear
we bawling
under the brunt of
free-trade hurricane
clinging like bad lizard to
ganga tree
changing colour
belly pon de ground when
hot iron come hovering
leaking conscience
like bamboo basket raking
foreign muddy bank
catching little action but
plenty talk
running wild like love vine over
any back
white or black

scrambling for greenback
morning after morning
still
waking up
stretching

Gun Talk

What
Yo gwine pull you gun
run she down
blow she to kingdom come
you ah stand yo ground
nar tek no wrong

Yes
Yo feel dat mek yo strong
mek yo man
but when yo done
yo gwine swallow a bullet
wid rum
chop off yo own hand
bun down the house
drink banana wine on ice

Sorry
me still nah see no don
no trojan
All me see ah one
sick
sick
man

Plain Talk

Ah know times rough
tings hard
you feel you gotta be tough
be bad
You don't want to be poor
or obscure
you want more
But hear me sing
Integrity is not a sin

So when they say you don't have to be broke
and try send you States wid a bag a coke
tell them you not for sale
Drugsman ah not for sale
When they offer you big wuk
then tell you to free up
tell them you not for sale
Bossman ah not for sale
Ah say ah not for sale

Most days Mammy got no money
Daddy
you can't find he
Nothing in de house to cook
teacher calling for more book
Head busting you can't rest
life look like one big mess
But hear my voice
There is great power in choice

So when they offer to set you up
tek you outta your little hut
tell them you not for sale
Bigman ah not for sale
When they pull up in big ride
tell you to drive on de side
tell them you not for sale
Vanman ah not for sale
Ah say ah not for sale

You feel strange in your own home
so alone
real helpless and small
invisible to all
restless and bored
your problems ignored
you want to bust out
But hear my shout
Inner strength is what it's about

So when they say them understand
and they go mek you a woman
tell them you not for sale
Homeboy ah not for sale
When they tell you dat you cute
then try destroy your youth
tell them you not for sale
Oldman ah not for sale
Ah say ah not for sale

All your friends out having fun
you chillin

dat does bun
They flamming in every fete
You ain't wuking yet
you can't rank style
you always looking wild
But in my words of gold
You still have a beautiful soul

So when they show you Nike and Fila
and all kinda Tommy Hilfiger
tell them you not for sale
Brandman ah not for sale
When they flashing big money
and bucket ah Kentucky
tell them you not for sale
Moneyman ah not for sale
Ah say ah not for sale

Long Talk
(from a Vincy jumbie)

Tonight ah come fuh rescue me culture
from all dem alien vulture
fuh tek back we Caribbean
in de name of Vincyland
fuh find de rhythm of conga and steel
and mek dem pulse in a way dat you
could feel

Tonight ah come fuh uplift colour
and give it dignity
reverse yo concept ah beauty
built on classic European style
show you dat Afro-Indo-Carib
sweeter by a mile

Tonight ah come fuh sing
de virtues of dis land
e ability fuh mek e people strong
fuh tell you dat nutten wrong
wid green banana and
coconut water
dat fresh fish beat frozen chicken
any time
and you could mek good good juice
wid lime

Tonight ah come fuh warn you
dat a home is not

a mansion of concrete
and stone
wid plenty room and
shiny furniture
dat nah wan home
not inna my picture
In a truly strong structure
pickney ah know dem puppa
are cherished
not banished
by dem mumma
there is respect and honor
for grandpa and grandma
and love live under dem shelter
even when no corn dey in de mortar

Tonight ah going whisper
and hope you go hear
ah secret dem who gone on
want me fuh share
Yo home ah de cradle
ah yo culture
Way yo nourish dey
ah way go come big later

Tonight ah come fuh freeze
foreign penetration
de invasion of lifestyles harmful
to we nation
fuh bruck dat tough jawbone
ah violence
and plug de leak
ah normal commonsense

Tonight me ah wind
and rain
me ah hurricane
flattening Americanism
ripping up materialism
exposing dem values
so shallow and thin
smashing de hundred ah mirror
dat muliply we colour
mimicking white culture

Ah come fuh challenge you tonight
fuh conquer de might
ah dat innocent TV screen
wid e own agenda
e dangerous scheme
Turn it round
mek it wuk fuh our side
fill it wid pictures of sound morals
and national pride

Tonight ah come fuh ask you
fuh think
fuh plan
embrace simple sincerity again
in dis land
Tonight ah invite you fuh rise up wid me
determined and strong
and reclaim we culture
we Caribbean

Bad Talk

He bin so hurry fuh leave
he mumma dirt yard
he pitch way she
hand-me-down sarbie
haul on he ha'penny larning
wipe de lamp black out he nose
grease de crack dem in he heel
and step up in the world

Now come see um
he can't find enough
crack and smoke
fuh haul up he nose
and down he throat
lay down naked as he born
pon de tough old truth dat
poverty never married
to dirt

Old Talk

Ten commandment pon
de ground
ah bearing up
and holding down
under progress
and tide tackling me
broadside
as me stand guard
over woodfire
bucket ah water
head-head pickney
flambeau and bashi
board beater pon river stone
clothes bone-dry before
you reach home
bush broom ah dirt yard
grass mattress
nah too hard
pail and posy
under bed
drum oven full
ah bread
Ah know me flour-bag world
ripping in de seam
but leaking and sagging
dis ah de playground
ah your grandmothers' dream

Sweet Talk

Hot water is a ting taste real bad to we
but add little sugar and
we drinking tea
Cold water and dry bread is jail food
we say
but put some sugar dey
and watch how juice appear
A lack ah sugar is no joke
in dis place
if yo war see riot
just bawl
sugar scarce

Some might look fuh call we
crazy sugar junkie
but deep inside we know
without dat sugar we got in store
we coulda a never endure
dem tough dry lie
and bitter indignity
heap high on de plate
ah we history

Back Talk

You could try hold me down
but you can't hold me back
cause I going way I going
in Jesus name
and it mek no sense
you turn over stone
looking for blame

Ley we just call it
technical failure
in every way
you can't interfere
wid de signal from
me soul to me ear
and me can't rewire
your life fuh mek
you understand
dat wings on a woman
don't mean horns
on a man

Just stand back
watch me go through
dat door
feet off the floor
ah catching a ride
pon any faint breeze
unleashed from
your pride
ah soaring wid ease

9781589398931